Napkin Folding

Napkin Folding

LINDA BARKER

SMITHMARK

Salamander Books Ltd., 1993
129-137 York Way,
London N7 9LG,
United Kingdom.

This edition published in 1993 by SMITHMARK Publishers Inc.,
16 East 32nd Street, New York, NY 10016.

ISBN 0 8317 1585 5

SMITHMARK books are available for bulk purchase for sales
promotion and premium use. For details write or telephone
the Manager of Special Sales, SMITHMARK Publishers Inc.,
16 East 32nd Street, New York, NY 10016. (212) 532-6600.

ACKNOWLEDGEMENTS

The publishers would like to thank
The General Trading Company
144 Sloane Street, London SW1
for the napkins, china and
glassware featured in this book.

CREDITS

Author: Linda Barker

Napkin designs by: Linda Barker

Managing Editor: Samantha Gray

Copy Editor: Alison Leach

Designer: Louise Bruce

Photographers: Graham Rae and Steve Tanner

Typeset by: BMD Graphics Ltd., Hemel Hempstead

Color Separation by: Scantrans Pte Ltd., Singapore

Printed in Singapore

CONTENTS

Introduction

6

INTRODUCTION

The Bow Tie's wavy effect is surprisingly easy to
achieve and looks most effective when displayed
on a decorative plate. Here, a silver napkin ring
complements a sea-green, linen napkin.

The use of table linen can be traced back to the Middle Ages when it was fashionable to cover the table with a linen cloth and, by the end of the 16th century, the wealthy classes had begun to sit down to huge feasts at a more formal, 'laid' table. However, at this time, people still ate with their fingers and, naturally, the ends of the tablecloths (along with pieces of bread) were brought into use for wiping greasy fingers and mouths. It was not unusual for a tablecloth to be changed several times during the course of a meal and, when laid diagonally, the corners of the cloth were even tucked into collars! The natural progression was to tablecloths with removable linen borders, eliminating the need to change the whole cloth.

The 17th century saw the introduction of forks and the penchant for lavish meals. It was at this time that the first type of napkin was used – initially a vast piece of linen, long enough to cover the flamboyant clothing worn by both gentlemen and ladies of the time, tied at the neck.

Decorative, folded napkins were introduced in the extravagant Baroque era, and there were some quite extraordinary examples. Napkins were folded to resemble birds, flowers and fans and, on particularly splendid occasions, a different creation might be provided for each guest. These ornate table decorations, some of them permanently cut and sewn into place, were often kept from one meal to the next with only the more simply folded ones actually being used. At the turn of the 19th century many of the more intricate folds remained in use, although these were generally kept for the ladies, a simpler fold being used for the gentlemen.

Today, we are more likely to see folded linen napkins in restaurants than in the home. However, with the use of attractive napkin rings and bands, there is no reason why a stylish napkin should not be a part of every well set table for any meal of the day. The more elaborate designs are sure to create a memorable impression at a dinner party or special celebration.

Basic Folding Tips

Creating a beautiful folded napkin is easy to do and there are only a few simple rules to follow and understand before successfully completing most of the folds in this book.

Firstly, ensure that hands and work surfaces are clean and always begin with an open napkin, placing it flat on the table in front of you. Try to fold on a cloth, as this will help the finished fold stand up.

When folding the napkin, always follow the directions carefully, bearing the following points in mind. If the directions tell you to fold 'down' into a rectangle or other shape, you should simply lift the edge of the napkin farthest away from you and fold it 'down' to meet the edge closest to you; do the opposite if you are instructed to fold 'up'.

The 'top edge' is the edge of the napkin farthest away from you;

similarly, the 'top point' refers to the angle farthest away from you. Sizes of napkins vary a good deal, but it is recommended that you don't use napkins less than 17 inches square. Napkins that are at least 20 inches square usually produce the best results and a dinner napkin, usually 26 inches square, is the ideal size to begin working with.

Cotton or linen napkins give the most elegant look and they fold best if freshly laundered, lightly starched and pressed. Napkins should be ironed flat and square at the corners. For the real perfectionist, napkins should be given a good soaking in cold-water starch and then mangled cold to obtain a stiff and dazzling quality. However, for the less committed, a can of spray starch gives very satisfactory

The Candle Fan looks dramatic unadorned,
or you could add artificial flowers to soften
the effect.

results, providing you do not use too much, or you may scorch the linen. Treated correctly, pure linen looks rich, takes folds well and is ideal for the more formal designs, while a cotton blend has a softer feel and lends itself well to more informal folds.

If you are fortunate enough to have lace napkins with decorative edges or embroidery, use folds that will show off their particular features. Many people like the look of delicate lace over a colored napkin; the two can be folded together for that extra special look.

If you prefer, all the designs in the book can be executed using paper napkins, usually available in cocktail and dinner sizes. Always buy the larger size and opt for the high-quality, thick type. If you can only obtain the cheaper, thinner variety, fold two or even three napkins together. Paper napkins can be suitable for even the most lavish of dinner parties when given the 'all star' treatment with elegant folding and the addition of a fresh flower or pretty ribbon. Solid color napkins are usually best to work with, as those with a design printed on only one side have to be carefully folded to ensure that the printed side faces outward on the finished design.

It is both fun and practical to have a variety of napkins of different patterns, colors and materials. Though you may not be fortunate enough to inherit lovely linen, your napkins will far outlast any piece of crystal or china. Generally, most spills and stains can be easily removed.

For that special event, it is worthwhile putting a bit of extra thought into the presentation of your napkin. Stenciled decoration can be applied with stylish results and thoughtfully planned designs can complement your crockery, your cutlery or even the food itself. A stenciled Chinese motif, for example, would help to make an Oriental meal really memorable. For special events and celebration meals, the napkins are always more than protection for diners' clothing – they are there to enhance and enliven even the most minimal table setting.

Above: Shown off particularly well in a conical glass, the Double Cornet makes a handsome display.

Left: You can make this pretty napkin ring by simply threading colorful beads on to thin elastic cord.

CHAPTER ONE

DECORATIVE DESIGNS

For special celebrations it's worth taking a little extra time to make up stylish
and unusual napkin designs. Bits and pieces around the house can come in
useful for creating imaginative table settings that everyone will remember.

Copy-cat Napkin Ring

1 Decorate some napkin rings to match your plates. You will need ceramic paints that match the colors of your china: in this case blue, green and pink. First, paint the outline of the design using a very fine brush and being careful to make a single sweeping movement with each stroke.

2 When the initial coat is dry, begin to fill in the outline with a second color, carefully following the design on your plate.

3 Finish off with a third and, if necessary, a fourth color, allowing each coat to dry before applying a new one. Protect the design with a coat of ceramic varnish. If you wish to decorate your table napkins too, follow the same procedure using fabric paints.

Lacy Napkin Folder

1 Here's a quick and simple way to dress up a plain napkin for an afternoon tea party. All you need is a square paper doily, slightly larger than the napkin and preferably in a contrasting color, and a floral motif. Begin by folding the napkin into a triangle.

2 Fold the doily diagonally. To create a 'spine' to allow for the thickness of the napkin, unfold the doily and make another crease about ⅜ inch below the first fold.

3 Cut out a floral motif such as a Victorian scrap and glue it to the center of the smaller (top) side of the doily. Insert the napkin.

Thanksgiving Napkin

1 This simple place setting is perfect for a Thanksgiving dinner. Use a sisal or straw placemat and a plain white napkin. For the decoration you will need a selection of dried flowers and grasses, and three lengths of beige ribbon, each about 20 inches long.

2 Tie the lengths of ribbon together at one end. Braid them until the braid is long enough to wrap around the napkin twice with a little left over to tie underneath.

3 Group the bunch of dried flowers and grasses together, securing them with thread or twine. Fold the napkin in half twice to form a long, narrow rectangle. Lay the flowers on top of the napkin. Wind the braided ribbon around the napkin and flowers twice and tie the ends under the napkin.

Lacy Napkin Bow

1 Ideal for a wedding or anniversary dinner, this lacy napkin bow is not only pretty but also easy to make. The napkins themselves should preferably have a lace detail around the edge. For each napkin you will need about 1 yard of wide satin ribbon and the same amount of insertion lace.

2 For the best results, the napkin should be starched and well ironed, and folded into quarters. To cut decorative points for the ribbon and lace, fold the ends as shown and cut them diagonally.

3 Fold under two corners of the napkin to overlap in the center, forming the shape shown here. Iron the folds flat. Lay the ribbon and lace flat, wrong side up, with the ribbon on top. Place the napkin on top and tie the ribbon and lace around it in a bow.

Festive Napkin Rings

1 Make some especially festive napkin rings for Christmas. Each one is made from a piece of cardboard tubing. Stick a strip of fake fur to the outside, to represent snow, and green felt to disguise the cardboard on the inside. Top it with a tiny green felt Christmas tree sparkling with sequins.

2 The leaf sprig ring is first covered with a strip of gummy-backed plastic. Cut the plastic wide enough to go over to the inside of the ring, and cover the inside with a thinner strip of ribbon. The leaf design with a red bow is a Christmas cake decoration.

3 Still another idea is to cover the ring with a small strip of wide satin ribbon. Glue a piece of narrower toning ribbon to the inside, folding the edges of the wide ribbon under as you go. Lastly, tie a strand of tinsel wire around the ring and finish with a bow.

Tassel Napkin Ring

1 This tasseled napkin ring is ideal for a special occasion. You will need two tassels and about 16 inches of cord per napkin, and a strong fabric glue. Attach the tassels to the cord by wrapping the loop around the cord and pulling the tassel through it.

2 Make the ring by feeding the cord through both loops of the tassels twice more. Make sure that the ring is large enough to slip easily over the napkin.

3 Using a strong glue, secure the ends of the cord to the back of the ring. Lay one end along the back and trim it. Having applied the glue to the inside of the ring as shown, wrap the remaining end over the cords, covering the trimmed end. Cut the remaining cord on the inside, and clamp in place until dry.

Floral Napkin Ring

1 This charming flower-trimmed napkin ring adds a touch of elegance to a table setting and is very easy to make. Bend a short length of florists' wire into a circle and twist the ends together to secure them.

2 Wind some very fine wire around one or two small silk flowers – chosen to co-ordinate with your china and table linen. Then twist the ends of the wire around the circle of florists' wire to hold the flowers in place.

3 Use narrow decorative braid to cover the wire. Hold one end in place with one hand, and use the other hand to twist the braid around the circle to cover it, beginning and ending underneath the flowers. Secure the ends with glue. Insert the napkin and add a fresh flower.

Stenciled Shell Napkin

1 You can easily decorate your own napkins with a stencil design to complement your china or decorative scheme. All you need is a plain napkin or a hemmed square of fabric, a stencil motif (either bought or original), a natural sponge and some fabric paint.

2 Position the stencil on the napkin. Mix the paint in a saucer. Dip the sponge into the paint and dab it on a piece of scrap paper to remove the excess. Alternatively, you can use a stencil brush, which will give a slightly different effect from a sponge.

3 You can either hold the stencil in place with your fingers or fasten it with tape. Dab paint through the stencil onto the fabric, taking care that it doesn't seep under the edges. When the paint is dry, fix it following the manufacturer's directions.

Golden Leaves

1 This is a very stylish napkin idea and is ideal for a special dinner party. You will need enough florists' wire to wrap around each napkin one and a half times. Paint or spray silk fern leaves gold, allowing two leaves for each napkin. Leave to dry completely.

2 Twist the ends of the wire around the stems of the fern leaves, securing them tightly, so that they can be curved easily.

3 Cover the wire completely using fine gold braid or ribbon. Twist tightly so the braid will not unravel and stick it down at regular intervals with glue. Twist the wire loosely around a rolled napkin with the leaves uppermost.

Stiffened Bow

1 This attractive napkin ring will add instant charm to any table setting. You will need a 36 inch ribbon for each napkin. Choose a ribbon to match your china. Cut the ends of the ribbon into points by folding them double and cutting a diagonal across the fold.

2 Coat both sides of the ribbon with fabric glue and tie a bow loosely around a glass bottle that has a diameter similar to that of the napkin roll. Leave until almost dry.

3 Slide the ring off the bottle and leave until completely dry. Insert a napkin that has been loosely rolled.

Ballerina

1 This is a pretty decoration for a little girl's birthday party and the clothespin dolls can be taken home afterwards. You will need the old-fashioned type of clothespin and non-toxic water-based paint. Each doll will need one pipe cleaner for her arms.

2 Pleat two small paper napkins into 'accordion' folds and fold each napkin in half. Construct the doll using the main photograph for reference.

3 Wrap two napkin skirts around each doll and tie them on securely with thread or fine ribbon. Finally, fan out the folds to give the effect of a ballerina's skirt.

Beaded Napkin Ring

1 This napkin ring uses those broken necklaces and loose beads and looks rather like a miniature bracelet.

2 Use thin elastic to thread the beads and knot the ends together securely. The rings should be big enough to slip easily over a rolled napkin. Make as many strands of beads as you like and secure the rings together by knotting across the width at regular intervals.

3 A dark-colored napkin shows off this beaded ring most effectively. Roll up the napkin neatly and insert into the ring.

Decorated Napkins

1 For the blue napkins, cut a star shape from a piece of cardboard – the cardboard must be slightly wider than the folded napkin. Hold the cardboard firmly in place over each napkin and spray gold or silver paint over the area. Let the paint dry for several minutes before you allow anything else to touch it.

2 A purchased stencil and oil-based stencil crayons are used for the decoration on the white napkins. Place your chosen design over the area you want to stencil. Rub the crayon over a spare area of stencil, then take the color up onto the brush and paint it over the stencil, in a circular motion.

3 Use the brush only over the parts you wish to show up in that color. Then switch to the next color. It is best to use a different brush for each color if you want a clear color definition.

Plaid Napkin

1 Use only three colors of fabric paint and decorate plain napkins to produce some stunning designs. Paint wide horizontal bands across a plain napkin, either freehand or using masking tape to ensure neater edges. If you prefer, make a paper pattern first to show the positions of the bands.

2 Paint vertical bands of the same width as the horizontal ones from top to bottom of the napkin, using another color.

3 Use a smaller brush and a third color to paint a fine stripe between the bands horizontally and vertically to complete the plaid napkin. When dry, fold the napkin as liked.

Ribboned Napkin Ring

1 This attractive napkin ring makes use of various lengths of ribbon that might otherwise be thrown away. Measure the circumference of a napkin ring and cut a pipe cleaner to this size. Wrap a length of ribbon tightly around the pipe cleaner, leaving a piece of ribbon free at each end. Secure the ribbon with thread.

2 Cover four or five matching lengths of pipe cleaner in the same way, using different colors of ribbon. Then sew each length together carefully to make a multi-colored band.

3 Shape the band round to form a ring and insert a napkin. Tie each ribbon securely, allowing the ends to curl as shown.

Jeweled Napkin Ring

1 This napkin ring will add sparkle to any table setting for a special occasion. You will need a small block of air-drying modeling clay, available at most art and craft stores. Roll out the clay and form it into a ring. A crown shape is shown in the photograph but you can sculpt any design you wish.

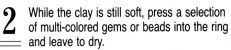

2 While the clay is still soft, press a selection of multi-colored gems or beads into the ring and leave to dry.

3 Paint the bare parts of the ring decoratively, taking care not to touch the gems or beads, and leave to dry. Brush the ring with acrylic varnish to protect it.

Net Napkin Ring

1 For a touch of frivolity, tie your table napkins in several shades of net. For each napkin cut three rectangles of different-colored net, 19 x 13 inch. Fold each piece crosswise into three equal sections.

2 Fold the napkin twice to form a square, and then fold it diagonally to form a triangle. Then roll it lengthwise.

3 Place the pieces of net on top of each other; tie them around the napkin and fan out the ends.

CHAPTER TWO

INFORMAL DESIGNS

Colorful and patterned napkins are ideal for informal designs – you
can even cut squares from fabric remnants (simply sew a hem around the
edges) or use paper napkins. With a little flair you can enliven a table
setting for any occasion.

Gingerbread Man Envelope

1 Sure to be a hit with children, each little gingerbread man is tucked into a napkin and has his own place card 'shadow'. Copy the shape of the gingerbread man onto stiff colored paper; set it aside. Using a length of narrow satin ribbon, tie a bow around the neck of the gingerbread man, leaving an end about 6 inches long to be attached to the place card.

2 Cut the ends of the ribbon into points by folding them double and cutting a diagonal across the fold. Cut the drawn shape from the colored paper.

3 Write the child's name on the shape. Apply a dab of glue and stick the card shape onto the ribbon. Fold back one corner of a bright-colored paper napkin to make an envelope for the gingerbread man.

The Triangle Pouch

1 The prepared napkins can be piled on top of each other or fanned out into a circle for a buffet meal. Fold the left- and right-hand edges inwards to meet in the center. Fold the top edge down to make a narrow rectangle.

2 Press the top right-hand corner and fold the bottom right-hand corner up slightly so it now touches an imaginary horizontal line.

3 Place a finger on the bottom right-hand corner and fold the top right-hand corner down to meet the bottom edge. Repeat the fold and tuck the last flap inside to form the pouch.

The Ruffle

1 Floral chintz napkins with this pretty fold are perfect for a summer tea party or luncheon outside. Fold the napkin in half left to right and in half again top to bottom. Place in front of you with the open corners pointing upwards.

2 Fold the first layer down and pleat it four times. Repeat with the second layer, placing this above the first layer of pleats. Press.

3 Turn the napkin so the pleats are vertical. Fold the napkin in half with the pleats on the outside and arrange on a plate.

Everyday Fold

1 This looks pretty on the breakfast, lunch or dinner table, with toast or a bread roll kept warm inside the pouch. Start by folding the napkin into three, then fold down the left- and right-hand edges as shown.

2 Turn the napkin over and roll up the two overhanging edges tightly to the base of the triangle. Fold across the center so that the rolled edges are on the outside.

3 Hold the napkin by the rolled section and squash the farthest part of the triangle across the diagonal and open out the napkin. Place on a plate.

Breakfast Fold

1 Let the children paint a section of a cardboard tube for the napkin ring and display the prepared napkin on a breakfast tray. Fold the four corners into the center and fold in half left to right and in half again bottom to top to make a small square.

2 Fold the top layer of the right-hand corner down and fold back the top left- and bottom right-hand corners, tucking them in neatly behind the napkin.

3 Press the sides back and slip the napkin through the ring until the lower flap just covers the top of the ring.

Envelope

1 Always popular with children, any number of treats can be hidden within the folds of this napkin. Adults might prefer a flower as shown in the main photograph! Fold the napkin in half across the diagonal, then fold the two outside edges into thirds along the lower edge.

2 Place a finger over the center of the napkin across all thicknesses and fold back the right-hand flap across the center, squashing down the triangular flap to make a small diamond shape as shown.

3 Fold down the top point of the napkin and tuck it into the diamond shape to close the envelope. Insert a flower if wished.

Bow Tie

1 This pretty fold is both simple and effective. Start by folding the napkin in half from left to right and in half again from top to bottom to form a square. Place the napkin in front of you with the open points to the left.

2 Starting at the bottom, pleat the napkin with 'accordion' folds of equal depth to form a strip that will fit into the ring.

3 Slip the napkin through the ring to the center and arrange the folds into a fan shape, as shown in the main photograph.

Oriental Fold

1 Almost like an origami fold, this design is simple to achieve and looks very stylish. Fold the napkin in half left to right and fold the top edge behind by only 1 inch. Place a finger at the center of the top edge and fold the left- and right-hand corners to meet in the center and form a triangle.

2 Fold up the bottom edge by only 1 inch to the front of the napkin and fold over the same edge to overlap the base of the triangle by 1 inch.

3 Hold a finger at the center point of this flap and fold together the left- and right-hand corners to form a second triangle. Fold behind the right- and left-hand edges to create a neat shape.

Circular Napkin

1 This original napkin fold has a bead and ribbon trimming. Paint a plain 1 inch wooden bead with a water-based paint to match your napkin. Allow to dry. Then paint on a pattern in a harmonizing or contrasting color.

2 Fold the napkin in half once along its length, and then pleat it accordion-style along its length, making sure that the folds are all exactly the same size.

3 Thread a length of narrow ribbon through the bead and tie it to hold the bead in place. Wrap the ribbon around the center of the napkin and tie it in a neat bow just below the bead. Fan the napkin out so that it forms a full circle.

The Sailing Boat

1 A smaller napkin may be used for this fold and it works equally well with linen or paper. Start by folding the napkin in half diagonally.

2 With the base of the triangle nearest you, roll the base up towards the top of the triangle. Roll as tightly as you can and stop rolling approximately 2½ inches from the top point.

3 Fold the napkin in half with the rolled edge inwards and arrange the boat on a plate with the edge extending over the rim.

The Waves

1 A simple fold that can be used at any time. Start by folding the napkin into three so you have a long narrow rectangle. Fold the left- and right-hand edges inwards, folding over twice on each side so that the edges meet in the center.

2 Turn the napkin over and fold in half from side to side. Then turn the napkin over again to reveal the 'waves'.

3 Slightly spread the three 'waves' apart. Small flower heads or menu cards can be tucked into the folds.

The Pineapple

1 A very simple, frilly fold which benefits from the addition of a pretty napkin ring. Start by pleating the napkin from top to bottom, accordion-style, making sure that the pleats are all the same size.

2 Holding the edges tightly, fold the napkin in half. Pull about two-thirds of the folded edge through the napkin ring as shown.

3 Push the ring over the napkin to within 2 inches of the open ends. Pull out the top folds to create the spiky leaves and plump out the base to make a nice fat pineapple shape.

Peacock's Tail

1 This design resembles the fan of a peacock's tail. Fold a square napkin in half from top to bottom so that the fold is at the top. Fold the right-hand edge over to meet the left-hand one as shown.

2 Keeping a finger on the center of the bottom layer, pull over the top layer of the bottom left-hand corner to form a triangle.

3 Turn the napkin over and pull over the top layer of the bottom right-hand corner to form a triangle. Fold the triangle in half and fan out the four points that have formed underneath, spacing them evenly. Place on a plate with the points facing upwards.

CHAPTER THREE

FORMAL DESIGNS

Impress your guests with a fabulous table display featuring formal napkin designs, ensuring that your meal has the best possible start. Most formal designs work well when made up with large napkins – choose the finest linen for intricate folds.

Lotus Blossom

1 This pretty design is not as difficult to create as it may appear. The technique is similar to that used in folding the origami 'fortune cookies' so popular with children. Lay the napkin flat, and begin by folding each of the four corners into the center.

2 Repeat this procedure, turning the corners inwards to make an even smaller square. Then turn the napkin over and repeat for a third time, holding the corners down in the center to keep them in place.

3 Still keeping your fingers on the center, reach under the napkin with your other hand to one of the corners and draw this outwards gently until it peaks out. Repeat with the other corners to form the petals. Draw out the four single-thickness flaps to make the sepals.

Pure and Simple

1 This elegant napkin fold is easier to achieve than it looks. An embroidered napkin with a scalloped edge is particularly suitable for this design. First fold the napkin in half diagonally, then bring the left- and right-hand corners up to meet at the apex, thus forming a square.

2 Turn the napkin over, and fold one corner up slightly as shown, taking care that the point is aligned with the apex.

3 Fold the left- and right-hand corners underneath the napkin on a slight diagonal, pressing the folds lightly in place.

Double Jabot

1 Fold the napkin twice to form a square and position it with the free corners at the top right. Fold the top corner back diagonally to meet the lower left corner, then turn it back on itself as shown. Continue to fold the corner back and forth to create a 'accordion' effect along the diagonal strip of napkin.

2 Lift the next layer of fabric from the top right-hand corner and repeat the procedure described in the first step to create two parallel strips with zigzag edges.

3 Pick the napkin up in both hands with the zigzag folds in the center. Fold it in half diagonally to form a triangle, keeping the pleats on the inside. Hold the right- and left-hand corners of the triangle and curl them back, tucking one into the other to secure. Stand the napkin upright on a plate as shown.

Pure Elegance

1 For best results use a crisply starched napkin to make this attractive fold which is a good choice for an elegant dinner party. First fold the napkin lengthwise into three to form a long rectangle. Lay it horizontally with the free edge away from you, and fold the left- and right-hand ends inwards to meet at the center.

2 Fold down the top right- and left-hand corners to meet in the center, forming a point. Hold the napkin in both hands and flip it over towards you so that the point is facing you and the flat side of the napkin is uppermost.

3 Lift the sides and pull them over towards one another to form a cone shape. Tuck the left-hand corner into the right-hand corner to secure it. Turn the napkin around and place it on a plate as shown in the photograph.

The Princess

1 Fold the napkin in half to form a crease along the center line. Then open the napkin out. Fold one half of the napkin lengthwise into three by bringing the top edge of the square inwards to the center line and then folding it back on itself as shown. Repeat with the second half.

2 Fold the napkin in half lengthwise by tucking one half under the other along the center line. Lay the resulting strip flat with the three folded edges facing you. Mark the center of this strip with a finger and fold the right-hand edge in towards the center and back on itself as shown. Repeat on the left-hand side.

3 Pull the top left-hand corner across towards the top right-hand corner to make a triangle, pressing down gently along the folds to hold them in place. Repeat with the remaining left-hand folds, and then do the same with all the right-hand folds. Ease the folds open slightly and display the napkin as shown.

The Bishop's Hat

1 This miter-shaped fold can be displayed either on a flat surface or in a glass, cup or soup bowl, which allows the flaps to drape gracefully over the sides. Begin by folding the napkin diagonally to form a triangle, then pull each corner up to the apex as shown to make a square.

2 Turn the napkin over so that the free edges lie towards you. Pull the two top flaps up and away from you; then fold the remaining two flaps back in the same way to form a triangle.

3 Turn the napkin over carefully, and pull the two outer corners together so that they overlap; tuck one flap into the folds of the other to hold them in place. Finally, turn the front of the 'hat' to face you, position the napkin upright and pull the loose flaps down to rest on the plate as shown in the main photograph.

Oriental Fan

1 This effective design benefits from a well-starched napkin. Fold the napkin in half lengthwise and then fold one end of the rectangle backwards and forwards in accordion-style folds, until just past the halfway point.

2 Holding the folds firmly together, fold the napkin lengthwise down the middle to bring both ends of the 'accordion' together. Keeping the folds in position in one hand, fold the loose flap of the napkin over across the diagonal.

3 Push the flap underneath the support as shown to balance the napkin and, letting go of the pleats, allow the fan to fall gently into position.

Double Cornet

1 This design looks best in a conical glass but can be adapted for a wider-based container. Although it takes a little more practice than most, it is worth the effort. First lay the napkin flat and fold it in three lengthwise. Position it as shown, with the free edge on top.

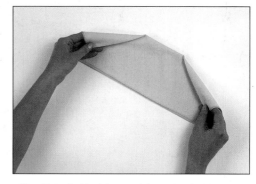

2 Take hold of the top left- and right-hand corners of the napkin with the index finger and thumb of each hand. Roll the corners diagonally towards you as shown.

3 Still holding the napkin, continue to roll the corners inwards in one sweeping movement by swiveling both hands and napkin down, up and over until your hands are together palms uppermost. By now the napkin should be rolled into two adjacent flutes. Place the napkin in a glass, arranging it neatly.

Pocket Napkin

1 This simple napkin fold is embellished with a few artificial flowers tucked into the pocket. Fold the napkin in half and then in half again to form a square; then fold it across the diagonal to form a triangle.

2 Position the napkin as shown with the four free corners uppermost. Working with the top layer only, fold it down several times to make a cuff at the bottom.

3 Fold the next (single) corner over so that the tip touches the top edge of the cuff. Fold the next two corners over to form three tiers. Then turn the right- and left-hand corners of the triangle to the underside and overlap them. Position the napkin as shown in the main photograph and insert the flowers in the top opening.

Lady's Slipper

 1 This pretty design is ideally suited to tea-time settings. Begin by folding the napkin into four – left to right, top to bottom – for form a small square. Then fold the four free corners back across the diagonal to form a triangle.

 2 Holding the napkin firmly at the apex, fold one of the outer corners over and towards you as shown, so that it overlaps the base of the triangle. Repeat with the second corner so that the edges of both flaps meet down the center of the napkin to form a kite shape.

 3 Turn the napkin over and fold the protruding flaps back over the base of the triangle. Then fold the triangle in half by pulling one of the corners over to meet the other. Holding both corners firmly together, turn the napkin upright and pull the four free corners upwards as shown in the main photograph. Arrange on a plate.

Four Feathers

1 This simple fold looks elegant placed in a wine glass. Lay the napkin flat. Fold it in half to form a triangle, with the folded edge towards you. Place your index finger on the center of this edge. Using the top layer of fabric only, bring the apex down to meet the left-hand corner.

2 Again working with the top layer only, bring the far corner down and across to the bottom left-hand corner.

3 Bring the remaining top corner down and across to the lower left corner as before, forming a triangle. Splay the folds slightly, then turn the napkin over so that the folds are underneath. Lift the edge and roll the napkin into a loose cone shape, stopping about halfway across. Fold up the bottom point and place the napkin in a glass, preferably one with a thick stem.

Candle Fold

1 This tall candle-shaped fold looks especially good if the napkin has a contrasting border. Lay the napkin flat. Fold it in half diagonally to form a triangle. Turn up the folded edge about 1¼ inch, then turn the napkin over so that the fold is underneath.

2 Beginning at the left-hand corner, roll the napkin carefully to form a cylindrical shape with the folded edge outwards.

3 Tuck in the end to hold the roll in place. Finally, fold down the front corner at the top as shown in the main photograph.

Pointed Pleats

1 This fold works particularly well with napkins that have scalloped or embroidered edges. Fold the napkin in half left to right and in half again top to bottom. Place the napkin in front of you with the closed corners uppermost.

2 Bring the layers up in tiers to meet the top point, leaving an equal space between each layer as shown.

3 Fold the left- and right-hand sides behind the napkin and stand the pointed pleats in a napkin ring.

Lily

1 This is a quick and simple way to create a stunning table display with the napkins attractively displayed in wine glasses. Begin by folding the napkin into four left to right, top to bottom so you have a square. Fold in half across the diagonal to form a triangle.

2 Turn the napkin so that the apex is away from you as shown. Starting at the bottom point, pleat from right to left.

3 Hold the base of the napkin firmly in one hand and insert in a wine glass keeping the pleats intact. Hold the top of the napkin and pull each individual pleat forward as shown to display the petals of the Lily.

Deco Fold

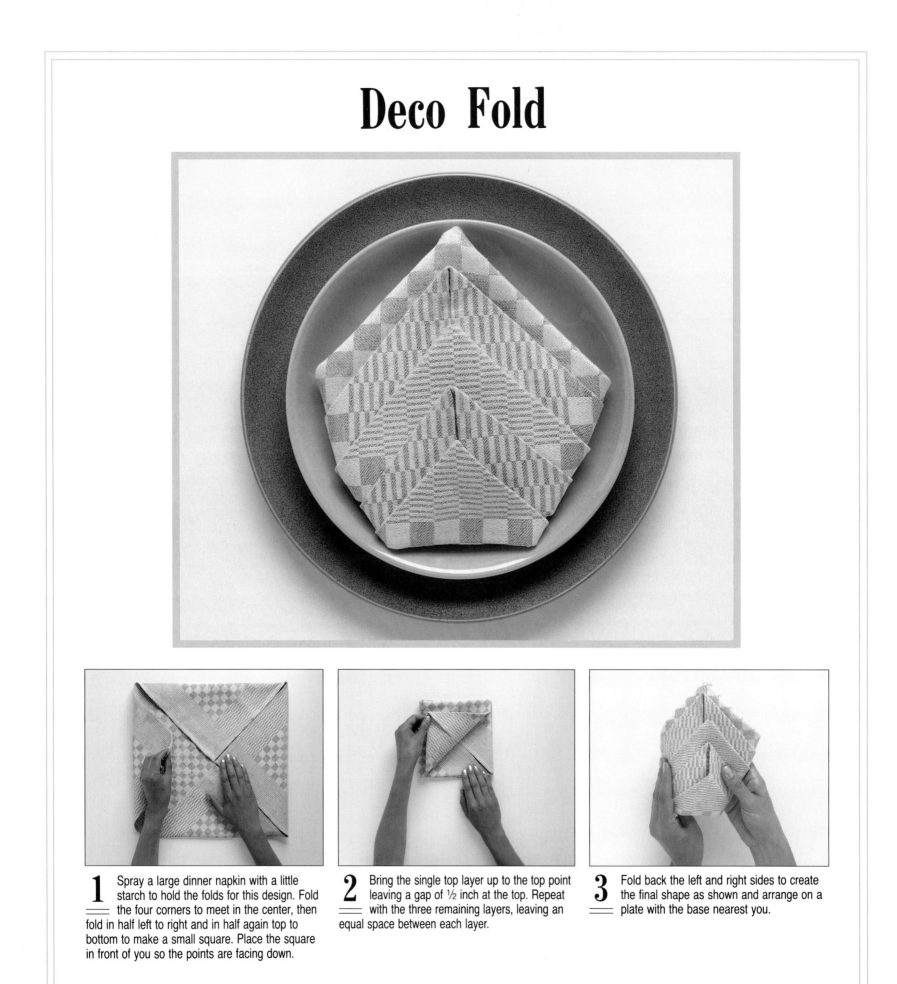

1 Spray a large dinner napkin with a little starch to hold the folds for this design. Fold the four corners to meet in the center, then fold in half left to right and in half again top to bottom to make a small square. Place the square in front of you so the points are facing down.

2 Bring the single top layer up to the top point leaving a gap of ½ inch at the top. Repeat with the three remaining layers, leaving an equal space between each layer.

3 Fold back the left and right sides to create the final shape as shown and arrange on a plate with the base nearest you.

The Umbrella

1 A crisply starched napkin is required for this very attractive fold. Pleat the napkin into six equal 'accordion' folds.

2 Tuck each fold in on itself at right angles and carefully press flat each triangular pocket that has been formed.

3 Hold the bottom left- and right-hand corners and fold the napkin across so that the two held points meet in the center of the napkin. Open up the folds and arrange the pleats outwards. Place the napkin on a plate and lay a flower in the center, if desired.

Miter

1 This decorative fold originates from origami. Start by folding the napkin in half, keeping the open sides to the top. Fold up the bottom left-hand corner and fold down the top right-hand corner until they meet in the center.

2 Turn the napkin over and position the long edges at the top and bottom. Fold the napkin in half and fold up the right-hand point from underneath.

3 Tuck the left-hand point inside the right-hand flap. Turn the napkin over and tuck the right-hand point into the left-hand flap. Open out the fold a little and position on a plate.

Candle Fan

1 It is best to use a large white starched napkin for this elegant design which may be decorated with fresh or artificial flowers, or a sprig of holly at Christmas. Fold the left- and right-hand edges inwards to meet at the center.

2 Place a finger firmly on the center of the napkin to hold the edges together and fold each corner back diagonally.

3 Tightly roll the top half of the napkin and pleat the lower half from bottom to top. Fold in half widthwise, place in a wine glass and gently pull out the folded pleats.

Palm Leaf

1 This stylish fold will benefit from a well starched napkin and the finest linen. Begin by folding the napkin in half diagonally.

2 Fold the left- and right-hand corners towards the center, leaving a gap of 2 inches between the inside edges. Fold up a 2 inch hem from the base and pleat from left to right across the napkin.

3 Set the base of the fold in a napkin ring or glass and open out the folds to form the palm leaf.

The Guard of Honor

1 This impressive design will hold tighter rolls if the napkin has first been well starched. Begin by folding both sides towards the center until they meet.

2 Place a finger firmly on the center of the napkin and fold each corner back diagonally to form projecting triangles.

3 Tightly roll the edge nearest to you up towards the center of the napkin, then roll the farthest edge down to meet the other roll in the center. Put a hand in the middle of the rolls, bend the napkin up at each side and interlock the four points. Finish by placing a bread roll or flower in the middle of the fold.

The Fan

1 This is definitely the napkin to impress! Start with a large, well starched napkin and fold the lower edge up towards the top edge, leaving a space of 2 inches. Fold up the new lower edge, again leaving a space of 2 inches.

2 Pleat the napkin from left to right, accordion-style, pressing the folds firmly each time.

3 Hold the napkin at the base and pull forward the edges on the bottom row where the pleats have been folded backwards, to make tiny triangular pockets. Continue along all the pleats on the bottom row and repeat the same process on the middle row, pressing the pockets. On the top row, fold the forward-facing pleats to make similar triangular pockets, facing backwards. Close the fan and press. Open the fan and arrange as shown.

The Butterfly

1 A crisply starched napkin is required for this pretty fold. Lay the napkin flat. Fold two edges to meet in the center as shown. Then fold the half nearest you across the center line and over on the top of the other half, to form a long, narrow rectangle.

2 Fold the right-hand end of the rectangle in towards the center, and with another fold double it back on itself as shown. Repeat with the left-hand side so that the double folds meet in the center.

3 Pull the right-hand back corner across to the left, bringing the front edge across the center line to form a triangle. Holding the right-hand side with one hand, use the other hand to fold the corner back to its original position, thus creating the 'wings' of the butterfly. Repeat the procedure on the left-hand side so that the napkin has two symmetrical wings you can arrange to look like the completed fold, shown above.

Index

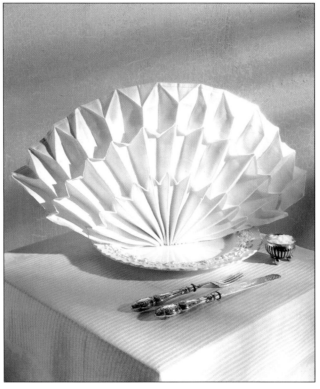